Seen God Lately?

RICHARD ADAMS

Seen God Lately?

With illustrations by David Whiting

London EPWORTH PRESS

7162 0385 5

Enquiries should be addressed to
Epworth Press,
Room 195, 1 Central Buildings,
Westminster, London SW1

Phototypeset by Input Typesetting Ltd
and printed in Great Britain by
The Garden City Press Ltd

Contents

Some of these pieces were broadcast under this title as late-night epilogues on Anglia Television. The author is grateful to Anglia Television for permission to reproduce them in this book, together with the illustrations produced by their Graphics Department.

Old and Young

Old age is cunning, creeping up on you when you're not looking, and suddenly staring you in the face one morning from the bathroom mirror.

'God,' I said, 'I look a hundred and four.'

'Rubbish,' said God.

'You here again?' I said. 'Whyn't you wait till I'm more awake?'

'Thought you needed cheering up,' he said. 'You're not old. You're not even forty.'

'I'm well on the way to senility,' I said. 'Just look at these bags under my eyes.'

'Wash your face,' said God. 'Shave that stubble off. You'll feel years younger.'

'That's just renovating the surface,' I said. 'My problem's deep down.'

'Go on,' said God. 'You're just feeling sorry for yourself. Wait'll you get to my age.'

'I'll wait,' I said, and rinsed the razor.

After breakfast, he was there again, waiting at the door while I heaved my coat on.

'I'll walk up with you,' he said. 'Sharp frost last night.' We passed front gardens full of wilting dahlias.

'They look like I feel,' I said.

'Just Monday morning,' said God. 'You'll be all right once you get to work and get stuck in.'

'That's just the trouble,' I said. 'The very thought of it wears me out. It's all getting up, working, and going to bed again. Where's the joy in that? Is that the prospect for another thirty years? No wonder I feel old!'

We stopped at the school gate.

'See you later then,' I said.

'I thought I might come in this morning,' he said. 'Have a look round.'

'Sure,' I said. As if I could have kept him out anyway. Not that I was always aware of his presence.

'You'll have things to do,' he said. 'I'll just wander round the classrooms.'

He padded down the long, bleak corridor and disappeared into Room Two. I put the lights on and went into the office to start unwrapping the papers and parcels of daily routine, then into my classroom, chalky and sunless.

'Mornin' Sir.'

It was Kevin, red-cheeked from the cold air, plump and bustling with a bag full of bubble-gum, football cards, and a toy mechanical digger to show me.

His delight was infectious. Sonya caught some of it as she came in.

'Cor, that's nice, Kevin. Let's have a go.'

She wheeled the digger along the desk top, scooping up a piece of chalk.

In ones and twos the rest drifted in, sharing their stories, news, jokes and new toys. When the bell went we settled down to sums and writing.

So the day passed, full of questions and answers – well, many questions, *some* answers. Involved in the children's enquiries, I found, here and there, an answer or two of my own.

I met God in the playground at the end of the day.

'Thought you were going to be around.' I said. 'Haven't seen you all day.'

'Really?' he said. 'Feeling better?'

'Yes,' I said. 'Funny how the day brightens when the kids start coming in.'

'Youth is infectious,' said God.

'Isn't old age?' I said.

'Yes,' he answered, 'but not when I'm around.'

'All in the mind, is it?' I said.

'And in the heart,' he said.

Match Points

They'd already kicked off when I got there. Wretched traffic! I was just in time to see a nice ball from the centre reach the left winger.

'Come on, Soggy,' I shouted. 'Cross it!'

'Come on *who*? said a voice over my shoulder.

'Soggy,' I answered. 'Look at him messing with it. Cross it man!'

'Soggy?' the voice asked again.

'His name's Crisp,' I said, 'Soggy Crisp. Suits him, doesn't it! Look at that. He's messed about with the ball so long he's lost it.'

'Shame,' the voice said. The ball went out of play then, so I glanced round.

'Oh, it's you God,' I said. 'How are you doing? All right?'

'Not so bad,' he said. 'You missed the first goal, you know.'

'Are we one up then?' I said.

'One down,' said God.

'I might have known,' I said. 'They get worse, this lot. I don't know why I keep coming.'

'Hey up,' said God, 'they're off again.' But the game didn't get any better. When it was over we walked home together.

'Not a bad game,' said God.

'What do you mean?' I said. 'We lost five-one.'

'The other side didn't,' he said. 'That's how it is, isn't it? Some you win, some you lose.'

'You can lose *so* many,' I said, 'and then it doesn't seem worth playing any more.'

'You need cheering up,' he said.' Come on, I'll buy you a brown ale.' So we called in at The Feathers and gave the match a thorough post-mortem.

'That's seven they've lost in a row,' I said. 'They're not worth supporting any more. I reckon I'll change clubs.'

'You're joking,' said God. 'You can't leave now, just when they need you.'

'Rubbish,' I said. 'I'll give my support to a team that wins now and again, not a bundle of all-time losers.'

'You won't find many all-time winners, either,' said God.

'What about top o' division one?' I said.

'They're the other end of the country,' said God. 'You can't support *them*!'

'I'll watch 'em on the telly,' I said. 'I can wear their colours and shout for 'em in my own front room. I'll support who I like.'

'From *that* distance?' said God. 'What makes you think they need *your* support when they're up at the top already?'

I began to suspect that he wasn't really talking about football any more. He's like that, is God; slipping odd, disturbing thoughts into your mind when you least expect it.

'All right,' I said. 'Never mind the football. I know what you're getting at. But you didn't make us all equal, did you? Some are born winners, some are born losers. You can't alter that, can you?'

'I could,' he said, almost to himself, 'if I wanted to.'

'Are you listening to me?' I asked him.

'Have you ever considered,' he said, 'that it takes a bigger man to lose a game than to win it?'

'What kind of cock-eyed philosophy is that?' I said.

'You think it's cock-eyed, do you?' he said, looking up at last and pointing a finger at me. 'Who talks about winning and losing, success and failure? Who measures success in pound notes and O-levels? *Who's* cock-eyed?'

'No need to get stroppy,' I said.

'I'll get stroppier yet,' he fired back. I'd never known him like this before, and there I was drinking beer he'd paid for.

'But God,' I said, 'listen to reason. You can't let people with talent go unencouraged, unrecognized. They've got to be given their chances, their rewards.'

'Exactly,' said God.

15

'Exactly?'

'I don't object to gifted people making the most of their gifts. It's why I gave them in the first place. They reap their own rewards.'

'So?'

He went on, 'It's when they think their talents make them superior to the unintelligent and inadequate. Then I *fume!*'

'Steady on,' I said. 'Steady on. Remember – Slow to anger and plenteous in mercy. . . .'

'Don't you remind *me*,' he said, 'when it's my so-called poor we're talking about.'

'Sorry,' I said, but he hadn't finished.

'They have their own level of achievement. Not inferior, just different, that's all. They achieve what they have the potential to achieve, and sometimes with a great deal more effort than brilliant minds ever need to call upon.'

'Oh, it's "Blessed Are The Poor" Day today, is it?' I muttered sarcastically. 'For theirs is the kingdom of God.'

'And why not?' said God. 'They *deserve* it.'

Growing Pains

I was singing in the bath:
>All things bright and beautiful,
>All creatures great and small.

It's a useful precaution when you've forgotten to lock the door.
>All things wise and wonderful . . .

The door burst open. 'Excuse me,' said a voice, 'Mind if I come in?'

Seeing it was God, I said, 'Be my guest,' and went on singing:
>The Lord God made them all.

'Is that the only one you know?' said God.

'That's a good old hymn, that is,' I said. 'One of the golden oldies.'

17

'Mmmm, bit selective, isn't it?' he said.

'There's a limit to what you can cram into seven verses,' I said.

'Write another,' he said.

So I said, 'Such as?'

'Well,' he began with a glint in his eye. 'What about something like . . . er. . . .

Dirt and smoke insufferable,
All slag-heaps great and small,
La da da di da di da,
Diseases cure them all.'

'That not funny,' I said.

'*You* used to sing it,' he said.

'I know,' I said, 'When I was a kid I used to sing it. I remember. My mother told me not to mock.'

'Quite right, too,' said God.

'But *you* were singing it,' I said. 'You're *God.*'

'All in the cause of truth,' he said.

'What's truth got to do with ugliness?' I asked. God padded over and perched himself on the edge of the bath.

'What's the matter?' he said. 'Lost the soap?'

I said, 'Never mind the soap, answer the question. Do you really want us to praise you for ugly things?'

'Ah!' he said, sloshing his hand about in the water. 'Here it is.'

'You're not listening to me!' I said. The wet soap suddenly shot from his hands and splashed back into the water.

'Whoops!' said God, and then resumed the conversation. 'The question is,' he said, 'did I or didn't I? – Isn't it?'

'Did you what?' I said.

'Create ugliness – or sorrow, or misery, or evil, or disease . . . Want any more?'

'That's plenty for the moment,' I said. 'But *did* you? *That's* the question.'

'Some I did, some I didn't,' he answered.

'Let's start with sorrow,' I said.

'Maybe,' said God.

'What do you mean, *maybe*?'

18

'Well, it exists, sure enough,' he said, 'like joy exists. But you can choose, can't you, whether to be sorrowful or joyful, whichever you fancy?'

'You mean, when a good friend dies I ought to dance and sing?'

'Why not?' said God. 'The dead wouldn't raise any objection.' There didn't seem to be any answer to that, so I tried something else.

'What about misery?'

'Same again,' said God. 'Human response to circumstances. You don't *have* to be miserable.'

'Well, I can see what you're getting at,' I said, 'At least, I think so. But when I think of the poverty and squalor. . . .'

'Ah, but you mustn't confuse physical comfort with spiritual well-being,' he put in quickly.

So I snapped back at him. 'Don't you care?'

'Yes,' he said. 'That's why there's always opportunity for those with plenty to restore the balance.'

'You've *always* got an answer,' I said. 'What about ugliness?'

'Can you name one thing in my world – that man hasn't interfered with – that's truly ugly?' said God.

There was a long silence between us then.

'You want to get out of there,' he said. 'Your water's cold.'

I ran some more hot in.

'Disease,' I said at last.

'You think it's ugly?' said God.

I paused – deliberately – contemplating an answer that might have been insight or just cussedness. Maybe I'd turn the tables on him for once.

'I think,' I said, 'disease is absolutely vital.'

'Tell me more,' said God.

'I'll show you,' I said, 'in the garden.' I stood up in the bath and reached for the towel.

'If you're going like that,' said God, 'I'd better warn the neighbours.'

When I'd dried and dressed, we went into the garden. The leaves were falling from the trees and clogging the dyke. Uprooted beanstalks, potato and beetroot tops lay with the grass cuttings on the compost heap.

'Change and decay,' I said to him.

'Well done,' said God. 'It's nice to know someone who's realized he's part of the natural order of things.'

'Thanks,' I said, 'but there's one thing that bothers me.'

He waited.

'Pain,' I said. 'Couldn't there be change and decay without pain?'

Quietly, he said, 'The explanation might be painful.'

'I'll risk it,' I said.

'For one thing,' he began, and his voice was firm, 'you eat things and do things which harm your body. And you *know* they do, but

20

you don't change your habits. The pain is self-inflicted. And it's a warning. Sometimes severe. It's the best I can do to warn you to take care, to abstain from self-indulgence. . . .'

'All right. Fair enough,' I said, 'Hint taken, though we don't always *know* what does us harm do we? But why mysterious and painful diseases?'

'Change and decay,' he answered. 'You said it yourself.'

'But the *pain*, God, the *pain*.'

He smiled, acknowledging my protest. 'You are funny,' he said, 'the way you like to tie ideas up in neat little parcels as though they had nothing to do with anything else.'

'What do you mean?' I asked.

'Pain,' he said patiently, 'belongs to the whole of creation. Because you hear terrible noises would you rather have no hearing? Because you see ugliness, would you rather have no sight? Because you sometimes feel pain, would you have feeling and sensitivity and tenderness taken away from you? Pain,' he went on, 'sharpens the edge of pity and compassion.'

'Oh, *come on*,' I put in, 'you can't justify pain because it provokes people to sympathy and good works!'

'Oh,' God said, innocently, 'I thought it was worth a try.'

'Well, you'd better try again,' I said.

'All right then,' he said. 'What about. . . .' And just for a minute he seemed to be weighing up in his mind whether he should tell me something or not. Then he said, 'Aren't you interested in sharing with me in the process of creation? The two of us working together?'

'But of course!' I said.

'Don't rush in, it's easier said than done,' he warned me gently, 'It's hard. It's birth, growth, survival. It's flowers forcing their way through trampled solid earth, straining for the light. It's trees baring their branches to the icy winds of winter.'

I considered the poetic imagery of his words and decided they were not enough. 'Sounds *almost* plausible,' I said, 'but it can't be the whole answer, can it?'

I thought I detected again a moment's hesitation before he answered, almost reluctance.

'The question of pain,' he said, 'preserves for me that element of mystery which makes men want to know me all the better.'

'Or not even bother,' I said.

He took me a little by surprise then, shrugging his shoulders and saying simply, 'Well, it's up to you.'

I said, 'God, I'd really like to know.'

He smiled. He seemed to be keeping to himself some secret he'd decided it wasn't yet time for me to share.

'Trust me,' he said, and a yellow leaf detached itself and fluttered gently down. Trusting, I knew that one day the Spring would come.

Body and Soul

I don't know why I went to the Disco really. Not my scene at all.

I couldn't complain. The cheese was good, and the French bread, and the white wine was excellent.

'But you can't stand the din,' said God, arriving unexpectedly and pulling up a chair. 'I see you've got the white wine. All right, is it? Fancied the red myself.' He took a sip or two and licked his lips. 'Not bad at all,' he said.

'Do they have to play it so loud?' I said. 'You can't hear yourself speak.'

'There's a table further down,' said God. 'Let's move.' So we picked up our glasses and took them to the other end of the hall, as far as we could get from the loudspeakers and flashing lights. The improvement was small.

'If you can't stand the noise, why do you come?' said God.

'It's in aid of charity, isn't it,' I said, 'I thought I'd give 'em my support.'

'You could've given 'em the money and stayed at home,' said God.

'Yes, but it wouldn't be the same, would it?' I answered, 'If we all thought like that, there wouldn't be a Disco at all. Gets people together, doesn't it?'

'Where two or three are gathered together. . . .' he quoted.

'There *you* are,' I finished for him, 'though I wouldn't have thought it was *your* scene either.'

'Where there's life . . .' he said.

'There's hope,' I added, wondering if that's what he intended, and if so, what he meant. 'All this jigging about,' I said. 'Seems so pointless.'

'They're enjoying themselves,' said God. 'What's wrong with that?'

'Oh, nothing I suppose,' I answered. 'It's just not my idea of enjoyment.'

'You old misery,' said God, 'Look over there, that'll cheer you up.'

He pointed to a tall, slim blonde in a long dress with no back. Not much front to it either. She was moving her young, attractive body to the beat of the music, her lips mouthing the words, her eyes sparkling with pleasure. I could have gone on watching her for a long time. I dragged my eyes away eventually.

'Very nice,' I said. 'Very nice.'

'You're *married*.' God reminded me.

'Spoilsport,' I said to him. 'Lead me not into temptation.'

'No harm in just *looking*,' he answered. 'After all, I made her the way she is. Gives *me* pleasure.'

It seemed to be a night for quotations. Must have been the wine.

'With my body, I thee worship,' God was saying. I nibbled a piece of cheese and waited for whatever was coming next. He asked, 'Know where that comes from?'

'Yes,' I said 'The marriage ceremony.'

'That's right,' he said. 'Where do *you* worship?'

'Worship?' I repeated, with an uncomfortable feeling his question was designed to lead the conversation somewhere I'd rather it didn't go, 'I worship at . . . um . . . well . . . High Street Chapel.'

'With your body?' he said.

I didn't know what he meant. 'You've taken that out of context,' I said. 'It's part of the marriage service, that's all.'

'I've taken it out of *your* context,' he answered, 'but not out of mine.'

'You've had too much wine,' I told him. 'You're talking drivel.'

'No,' he said, 'it's all this Disco music numbing your brain. Let's go outside. The fresh air'll clear your head.'

In the car park we surveyed the vast expanse of dark sky, the bright moon and stars. We talked about creation.

'And then I made *you*,' said God, 'body, mind and spirit. Would you agree that you use your mind and spirit when you worship in your little chapel?'

'And at work,' I said, 'during the week. I'm not one of your Sundays Only Brigade.'

'I'm very glad to hear it,' said God. 'In that case I shouldn't need to tell you that you can worship me with your *body*.'

'Oh?' I said.

'By the sweat of your brow, by the toil of your hands, by the application of sinew and muscle,' he went on.

'You make it sound like hard work,' I said.

He sighed. 'You're dimmer than I thought,' he said. 'What's to stop you offering me your leisure as well?'

I couldn't think of anything.

'Well, come on in then,' said God, almost skipping back to the dance hall. The pounding music poured through the doorway. By the time God reached it he was writhing and jigging better than any of them.

'Come on then!' he shouted. 'Join the congregation!'

Train of Thought

Snug with a good book in a corner of an empty compartment, I was on my way to London by the 8.32 from Thorpe Station. Suddenly the door slid open.

'Morning!' a voice said.

I didn't look up. The book was really good.

'Nice day,' the voice said above the clatter of suitcases as he heaved them onto the rack. 'Going up to the city, are you?'

What was the use? I couldn't ignore him. I shut the book.

'Oh, it's you,' I said.

It was God, sitting opposite me now, grinning as usual. 'Do you have to keep following me about?' I said. 'I can't go anywhere.'

'I'm sorry if I'm not welcome,' said God, but he didn't look it.

'You're an invasion of privacy,' I said.

He grinned again. 'You can't be private on a public railway.'

'Not anywhere, where you're concerned,' I said. 'Not even when I'm alone. *You* have to be there, stirring about in my head, prodding and poking.'

'You make me sound like a brain surgeon,' he said.

So I snapped back at him, 'Can't you be serious for one minute? If you will insist on living in my head, prompting or checking my actions, disturbing my thoughts and emotions, you might at least do it with a straight face. I don't know whether I'm coming or going.'

'Course you do,' said God, 'You're going, aren't you?'

I said, 'What?'

'To London!' he added.

'And I suppose I've got to put up with that sort of humour all the way, have I?'

'No,' said God, leaning forward to look me right in the face and speaking as though in capital letters. 'Let's have a deep and searching theological discussion.'

'You're making fun of me,' I said. 'You know all the answers, it wouldn't be fair.'

'Never mind,' he said. 'I'm getting out at Colchester anyway.'

There was suddenly a cold draught in the compartment, so I got up and shut the window.

'You're not going all the way then?' I asked, trying not to sound disappointed.

'Not if you want to go it alone,' he answered. 'I know when I'm not wanted.'

'I didn't mean it like that,' I said. 'It's just that. . . .'

'Train's slowing down,' he said. 'Must be nearly there.' He stood up and reached for his cases.

'Do you *have* to go?' I said.

'What *is* it you want?' he said, but I suspect he knew really.

'Answers,' I told him. 'Just a few. If you're going to haunt me for ever, I'm entitled to one or two answers, aren't I?'

28

'Such as,' said God, settling back in his seat again as the train picked up speed.

'Such as: What's right? What's wrong? And: What's life for?' I said.

'They're not answers,' said God, 'they're questions.'

'You exasperating old man!' I said. 'You haven't *got* any answers, have you?'

'No,' he said, his face giving nothing away. So I pressed him a little harder.

'Then how can you be in control?' I asked him. 'All-powerful, all-knowing, all-seeing God?'

'Who says I'm in control?' said God. 'Only *you*!' But there was a twinkle in his eye. Just testing, I thought. Or was he?

'You believe,' he went on, 'that I'm a God who lives in men and women; yet you still cling to the old idea of *remote* control, the imposition of my will on yours from afar, my hand interfering in human affairs to make sure my plans turn out all right. That's not control.'

'What is it then?' I asked.

And he said, 'Prison and death. My kind of control is more subtle.'

'Yes,' I said. 'So subtle it's non-existent.'

'If it didn't exist, you wouldn't complain about it,' he said, 'I've heard your prayers when you've had problems. You don't like having to make decisions. You want *me* to make them for you.'

'No, not really,' I said, but it was pointless trying to convince God, when I wasn't at all sure myself.

'*Not really*?' he repeated. 'Well, stop moaning then. Learn to choose. Freedom or prison, which is it to be? I'm not here to make decisions for you but to help you face the consequences of the ones you make yourself.'

The train had stopped. He got to his feet, took down his suitcases, shook me by the hand, and was gone.

I couldn't settle to the book again. I just sat there, feeling rather empty.

As the train began to move off again, the door of the compartment slid open and I saw that God had come back.

'Changed your mind?' I said.

'No, *you* did,' he said cryptically.

Before I'd worked out what he meant, he said, 'Asked any good questions lately?'

'There'll always be plenty of those,' I said, 'while you're around.'

'And as long as there are questions,' he replied. 'I'll be around.'

Spilt Milk

I'd missed the bus, with half an hour to wait for another, so I went for a cup of tea and a bun in the Bus Station Cafeteria; sat by myself at the window.

Now what made me do that?

There was an old man sitting in the corner clutching a violin case and watching the buses rumble by. There was another, much younger, tucking into a meat pie. I could have sat with one of them. Still – perhaps they preferred to be alone with their own thoughts. Who was I to intrude?

'Quite right,' said God. He'd come in without my noticing and brought his cup of coffee to my table.

'Don't you think we're a funny lot, though,' I said, 'the way we ignore one another?'

'Yes,' he said at once.

'Thanks very much,' I answered.

'Well,' he said, 'You *did* ask!'

He drank some coffee and waited, clearly expecting me to say something else.

'There must be a thin line,' I said at last, 'between taking an interest and interfering.'

'That's right,' he said, 'People often need help, but if you wait for the right moment you might be too late; step in too early and they tell you to mind your own business.'

'You're absolutely right,' I said.

He went on, 'You can't offer a helping hand without undermining people's independence, that's the trouble.'

'Yes,' I agreed. 'Independence.'

'You're just as likely to get a smack in the face,' he said, 'whichever way you tackle it.'

'Must be a social worker's nightmare,' I suggested, 'I don't know why anyone bothers.'

'Well,' said God, 'people expect to do themselves a bit of good. Kindness bringing its just reward and all that.'

'Huh! Fat chance there is of that happening,' I said, 'if no one admits to needing help.'

'No use crying over spilt milk,' said God.

'*Spilt milk?*' I asked. 'What's that got to do with it?'

'No use crying if nobody's spilt any either,' he went on.

'Don't talk in riddles,' I said, 'I don't follow you.'

'You do-gooders are all the same,' he said with a totally straight face, 'feeling deprived, just because there isn't any mess or disaster for you to mop up.'

'I see,' I said, irritated. 'You're just trying to provoke me.'

God looked thoughtful for a minute, examining the dregs at the bottom of his coffee cup. Then he looked up. 'Do you know?' he said, 'I've just drunk this coffee without any sugar.'

Some days he's hopeless. 'I don't know why I talk to you,' I said.

'You want to be of some use in this world and nobody can tell you where to start. If you do get a chance to help somebody, other folks think you're only doing it for your own ends. You can't win.'

'Who wants to win?' said God.

'I do!' I said. 'If I can't have gratitude, surely I'm entitled to a bit of satisfaction, aren't I?

'It's not winning that matters. . .' he began.

'Oh, I know,' I interrupted, 'It's playing the game. Twaddle!'

'Twaddle?' said God, unperturbed, 'What a jolly word. Say it again.'

'Twaddle!' I repeated, getting up, 'I can't stay here all day, arguing with you. I've got a bus to catch.'

'Me too,' said God.

It was time for the old man with the violin case to catch his bus too. We all got to the door together and I held it open for them both.

The old man was struggling with a bag of shopping as well as his violin. Suddenly the bag gave way. Tins and packets tumbled down

the steps. A bottle of milk rolled across the cafeteria floor spilling its contents in a crazy trail beneath the tables. I shot a glance at God, but he was already outside rescuing a tin of carrots from under the wheels of a bus.

I sat the old man down, borrowed a cloth and a brush and dustpan. The mess was soon cleared up and the girl behind the counter found another bag for the old man's groceries. He said how grateful he was as we put him on his bus.

'That's all right,' I said. 'Glad to be of service.' I turned to God. 'Weren't we?'

'Yes,' said God. 'Fancy another cuppa?'

'Not now,' I said. 'I'll go and get my bus.'

'I wouldn't be surprised,' he said, looking down the slope of the bus station towards the exit, 'if that one wasn't yours.'

34

He didn't try to conceal his amusement. I watched the double-decker vanish round the corner.

'All right,' I said. 'You win. I'll take the consolation prize.'

'What?' said God.

'Just for that,' I grinned, 'you *can* buy me another cup of tea!'

Up the Workers?

The factory gates were shut, with a crowd of workers guarding them. The handwritten placard spoke for itself:

OFFICIAL PICKET

I was more than surprised to find God standing there with the pickets, warming his hands by a fire they'd made in an old oil drum.

'You?' I said.

'On strike,' he said.

'But *you*, God, of *all* people,' I said, 'You can't take sides. You're supposed to be impartial.'

37

'Oh, but I *am*,' he said, pointing through the bars of the gates. At an upstairs office window I could see his identical likeness looking down, frowning at the picket line.

I blinked and looked again, but he was still there. I turned to the God by the oil drum.

He chuckled. 'You know me,' he said, 'I get everywhere.'

'But you can't be on both sides at once,' I protested.

He chuckled again. 'I'm not. Look out. Here I come!'

An articulated lorry was turning into the entrance. At the wheel . . . guess who?

'This is ridiculous,' I said, as God and the body of pickets moved forward to flag God the lorry-driver down. There was a brief conversation between God the picket and God the lorry-driver who nodded, shrugged, put the lorry into reverse and drove away.

I confronted God the picket with the nonsense this whole situation was. 'What do you hope to achieve?' I said. 'Talking to yourself?'

'*You* do it,' he answered. 'You used to say it was the only way to get a sensible answer.'

I ignored that. 'What are you striking for?' I said.

'I'll give you three guesses,' he said.

'Money!' I answered.

'Oh,' said God, feigning disappointment, 'you guessed.'

'There must be something you can do without going on strike,' I said. 'You're cutting off your nose to spite your face.'

God rubbed his nose thoughtfully, 'Tell me more,' he said.

'Go on long enough,' I explained, 'and you reduce the profits from which your wages are paid, and ruin the reputation of the firm 'cos you don't meet your delivery dates.'

I said, 'Listen. You've stopped that lorry-driver doing his job; that bloke up there in the office has nothing to do but wonder when work'll get back to normal. You're mucking about with other people's freedom. It's criminal.'

'Rot!' said God, 'Solidarity, that's what it's called.'

'And what for?' I asked him, 'Go on like this, you'll have no job to go to.'

'Rot!' said God again, 'Let them sack us if they dare. We'll take the factory over, stage a work-in. A man's got a right to work.' He paused. He must have been aware that his arguments had now turned full circle, but he let it appear that it had taken him by surprise.

'Oh!' he said at last.

'Precisely,' I said, with a feeling there was something very odd about the conversation. There was I putting God right. I wondered how many times I'd done it before without realizing it. I wondered, too, how often he'd set out to make me think by deliberately setting up the opposition.

'Hey up!' said God. 'Here we go again.'

A bus full of office workers had pulled up in the road and the driver with his head stuck out of his cab was wondering whether to turn in at the entrance. The bus-driver's face was more than familiar.

'It's *you* again!' I said to God the picket, but he was busy, leading the other pickets forward, brandishing their fists and placards, and shouting.

The event had taken on the proportions of a nightmare. The faces at the windows of the bus were all the same too – God's face, though with different expressions, some curious, some confused, some plainly frightened.

They got through in the end, the driver taking his life and theirs in his own hands and driving straight at the shut gates which opened with a crash to a chorus of jeers from the pickets.

I stood by the fire, wondering where it would all end. Suddenly God emerged from the chaos and strode across to me. 'What do you think of that?' he said.

'My old dad was right,' I said. 'He used to say – This country's full of willing people; half willing to work, and the other half willing to let 'em.'

'Livens up a dull morning,' said God.

'You must be joking,' I said.

'Yes,' he said, suddenly very serious, 'I've had enough of this. Let's go and put the kettle on.'

I took him home.

'I quite like a Marie biscuit,' he said, sitting with his feet up. 'Nice cup o' tea an' all. I can *do* with it.'

'How'd you get mixed up in all that sordid business?' I asked.

'You know me,' he said, 'I have to see everybody's point of view. My life's in people.'

So I said, 'That's the Kingdom, is it? What's happened to the power and the glory then?'

He supped some tea and then stared broodily into the mess of leaves at the bottom of his cup.

'Don't talk to me about power,' he said. 'You've seen for yourself how that gets used. That's why there isn't any glory. Not for me, nor for anybody else.'

He was quiet then for a long time. I had never thought of God ever being hurt or dispirited, but even if he was only pretending, his performance was utterly convincing. There was no doubting he was tired and sad.

'More tea?' I said.

'No thanks,' said God, 'I was just sitting here wondering . . . what would happen if I really did go on strike?'

Collision

On my way home the sun was warm through the car windscreen, the sky was clear blue and the road ahead open and straight. It was one of those days when life, for once, seemed worth living, full of sunshine and promise. God was in his heaven and all was right with the world.

And then the van that I thought was parked by the roadside pulled out unexpectedly as I was overtaking.

He was bigger than I was. When the police had come and gone, he drove away in his van with only a dent or two. I just leant miserably against my heap of wreckage and waited for the breakdown truck.

I didn't need to tell the driver what had happened. He knew. But then – God would.

'*You* again?' I said, surprised, yet not surprised when I thought about it. God viewed the battered remains of my car.

'You've dented it slightly,' he said with a grin.

'Don't be funny,' I said, 'I've wrecked it – written it off completely. What am I going to do now?'

'Get another?' said God.

'What with?' I said. 'Buttons? You know I'm hard up. Couldn't have happened at a worse time.'

'Rubbish!' said God. 'You don't know what it is to be hard up.'

'Do you?' I said.

'The whole world's poverty is mine,' he said. 'You can't be harder up than that.'

'Now you're just trying to make me feel guilty,' I said.

'I'm just saying you could be a whole lot worse off,' said God 'Come on, let's tow this junk away.'

He hooked up the car, all bent and buckled, and we climbed into the truck.

'I'll take you home,' he said.

'Thanks,' I said, 'I was having a good day till this happened. Why'd you have to pick on me?'

'On you?' said God. 'What makes you think you're so special?'

'Precisely,' I said. 'There's a million other motorists you could have picked on. Why *me*?'

God was quiet for a minute as though he was gently absorbing the noise of my protest.

'That accident,' he said at last, 'was either your fault or the other bloke's.'

'It was *his*!' I said.

'I'm not taking sides,' said God, 'but I'm not taking the blame either.'

'I suppose you're right,' I said, 'I'm sorry. I had to shout at *somebody*.'

'S'just reaction,' said God. 'Only natural. I quite understand. How's your knee?'

44

'How'd you know about that?' I said.

God smiled and tapped the side of his nose with a long forefinger. Of *course* he knew. Well, he *is* God.

'It hurts,' I said. 'Scraped the skin off on the dashboard. Very tender.'

'You wait until tomorrow,' he said. 'Bang like that shakes you up. You'll find aches and pains in bones and muscles you didn't even know you'd got.'

'Some comfort *you* are,' I said. 'Can't this truck go any faster? I want to get home.'

'You'll get home,' he answered. 'Can't go any faster when I'm towing. Might damage the load!'

'Now you're adding insult to injury,' I said.

'*What injury?*' said God, suddenly fierce. '*Injury!* One scraped knee when you might have been a mangled corpse? If you're suffering from shock tomorrow, it ought to be the shock of being alive!'

'What's that supposed to be?' I said. 'A plea for gratitude?'

'*You* work it out,' said God.

So I did. When we stopped, I watched him unload my wrecked car at the garage – the whole front of it caved in, buckled and broken.

It could have been me, buckled and broken.

The old words were still buzzing in my head, but they were asking a different question. I was alive . . . *Why me?*

Up the Polls

I was loading bundles of old newspapers into the car when I heard the loudspeaker van bleating incomprehensibly three streets away.

Jack next door, trimming his hedge with a pair of blunt shears, said, 'What's all that about then?'

It wasn't any clearer when the van came round the corner into view.

'God knows,' I said. Turned out I was right.

God stopped the van and wound the window down. 'Nice to see you again,' he said. 'Going to vote for me?'

'I like to know what I'm voting for,' I said.

So God said, 'Here. Have a leaflet.'

It had a single sentence on it: *Blessed are the poor.*

'I see,' I said. 'Socialist, are we? I thought you weren't supposed to take sides.'

'Quite so,' said God, getting out of the van, and he swapped the leaflet for another. This one read: *Blessed are those who hunger and thirst for that which is right.*

'Conservative then?' I asked him.

'Wrong sort of right,' said God. 'Try again.'

'What's left?' I said. 'Only the Liberals.'

'They're not left,' he said, 'They're somewhere in the middle, aren't they?'

'You're just playing games,' I said, 'Being all things to all men. Politics is a serious business, you know.'

'Oh yes,' said God, 'I'm serious.'

So I said, 'You oughtn't to get mixed up in politics at all. All that lust. . . .'

'That what?' said God, eyes twinkling.

'All that lust for *power*, I was about to say.'

'I know,' said God, and shuffled through his leaflets to find another. *Blessed are the meek*, this one said.

'The *what*?' I exploded. 'The *meek*? You don't find many of those in politics. The *ambitious* maybe!'

'Ambitious for what?' he asked, and recited a list of possibilities for me to choose from. Power, position, money, fame, popularity. . . .

I stopped him there. 'Popularity? In politics? They're lucky if they're not torn to shreds by the papers and the telly. Just because they're in the public eye, even their morals are supposed to be superhuman. *Everyone* thinks he knows better than the politicians.'

'So glad you've noticed,' said God. 'Have another leaflet.'

'I'm trying to give them up,' I said. 'They're bad for the brain. What's this one then?'

He pushed it towards me: *Blessed are you when men revile you and persecute you and utter all kinds of evil against you on my account.*

'In politics?' I said again, 'Who takes any account of you?'

He looked me up and down and seemed a little disappointed. 'I

thought you knew better than to cast doubt on the sincerity of the many by pointing to the hypocrisy of the few,' he said.

'Sorry,' I said, but he wasn't finished.

'I belong as much in the corridors of power as anywhere,' he went on, 'I know the problems too. Do nothing, folks complain. Do wrong, they condemn. Do good, they criticize. The public's never satisfied.'

'What's that meant to be?' I said. 'Complaint or commendation? You know how being satisfied can breed complacency and hinder real progress.'

'Every one a little gem,' he said. 'You should be writing these.' He pushed yet another leaflet at me: *Blessed are those who hunger and thirst after that which is right, for they shall be satisfied.*

'You've given me this one before,' I said, 'Come to that, I've heard 'em all before. Sermon on the Mount. Matthew's Gospel, chapter five.'

'Bingo!' said God.

'Doesn't say when,' I pointed out.

'When what?' said God, as if he didn't know.

'When they'll be satisfied – these people who hunger and thirst after that which is right. You're just like all the others. Nothing but promises.'

'Really!' said God, 'How d'you expect promises to be kept without the support of the people? Have a little faith, *please.*'

'In what?' I asked, 'One pencilled cross against an unknown name. One vote for God knows who. It's like leaping in the dark.'

'You're right,' said God, 'I know who. And that's what faith is for. Not making decisions, *facing* them.'

He got in his van and slammed the door. As he drove away, I saw the poster on the back. Another little gem: *Have faith, move mountains,*

Promises, I thought, always promises. Or maybe, I thought again, I'd given him my vote and not my heart.

Getting Through

The letter flopped on to the mat like a dead bird, adding yet another black day to a black year.

'It's just one damned thing after another,' I said to no one in particular. But I wasn't alone.

'What's up?' said God.

'You know what's up,' I said, flapping the letter at him, 'You know what it says, don't you?'

'Dear Mr Adams,' he said, quoting from memory, 'Regarding your proposed purchase of 84 Theobald Terrace. . . .'

'All right, all right,' I said. 'No need to prove it. I know you know.'

'And I know you know I know,' he chanted.

'Shut up,' I shouted. 'Stop being so infuriating and *do* something.'

'Such as?' he asked.

'Get things moving,' I said. 'I should have moved into this house *weeks* ago. The kids could have been settled into school, and I'd not be forking out a fortune travelling to work and back. Have you *seen* the price of petrol?'

'Sorry,' said God, but it didn't sound like much of an apology. 'I can see this is going to be a long session,' he added, 'I'll put my feet up if you don't mind.'

So I followed him into the front room where he rearranged the cushions on the settee and sat with his legs stretched out along the whole length of it.

I was still holding forth: 'First we find a house that's just what we want, but what then? Subsidence! So we look for another, only the surveyor reports that has subsidence too. And all the surveys and paperwork losing us precious time.'

'Do stop waving that letter about,' said God. 'It's causing a draught. And *do* sit down!'

I didn't sit down. He was taking it all so calmly I could have *clouted* him.

'You just don't care do you,' I said. 'The minute we find a house that isn't actually falling down, you mess things up again. *Legal complications*! Missing deeds and God knows what!'

'*Exactly* what,' said God, 'Go on.'

'I'm sick and tired of it,' I said. 'Enough is enough. I swear you do it on purpose.'

'Victimization,' muttered God.

'It's victimization,' I said, 'Why don't you leave me alone? Go and interfere with somebody else for a change.'

'It's not fair,' he muttered.

'It's just not fair,' I said. 'All I wanted was to move house, nearer my new job, make life so much easier for us all.'

'It's not too much to ask, is it?' said God, as I snatched a quick breath.

'Is it *too* much to ask?' I said. '*Is* it?' Then his mutterings-in-between finally registered. 'Hey! What game do you think you're playing?' I said.

'Housey, Housey?' God suggested.

'Oh stoppit, stoppit, stoppit!' I shouted. '*Enough!*'

'Oh dear,' said God. 'Seems to be a breakdown in communications somewhere. Shall I go and make a pot of tea?'

'I don't want *tea!*' I yelled at him, 'I want some *action!*'

'You've had nothing *but*,' he said, getting up. I followed him into the kitchen.

'Action?' I said. 'What action?'

He filled the kettle and plugged it in. 'Months of it,' he said. 'House agents, solicitors, building society managers, surveyors, structural engineers – a cast of thousands. Cecil B. DeMille didn't have many more when he made *The Ten Commandments*.'

'I don't know why I bother with you,' I said. 'All these months without a proper answer.'

'Rubbish!' said God.

'There was that super house in Lionel Road,' I said.

'Falling down,' said God. 'Even the mice wore tin helmets.'

'You needn't make fun,' I said, 'It had potential, that house. It was cheap. We'd have had the money to spare to repair it, modernize it, make it *ours*.'

'You hadn't the time or the energy,' said God. 'You'd a new job to see to, and you weren't well either.'

'Well you might have said so at the time,' I shouted. 'It's all this hanging about that's so annoying.'

'You wanted me to spell it out for you?' God said. 'I would have thought the answer was plain enough. It was *No.*'

'The kettle's boiling,' I said.

'You spin your prayers from the threads of dreams,' God said. 'My answers are spun from reality.'

'I'm sorry,' I said, 'And I'm sorry I shouted at you.'

'That's all right,' said God. 'I'd sooner you shouted than stopped communicating. Have a cup of tea.'

Black Prospects?

I was raking up and shovelling out last autumn's leaves from the dyke at the bottom of the garden.

'If you'll lend me a pair of wellies,' said God, 'I'll give you a hand.'

'What do you want with wellies?' I said. 'You're God. You've got waterproof legs.'

'That's right,' said God. 'Like yours.'

I said, 'Oh yes, s'pose I have.'

'Another miracle you take for granted,' he said. He hitched up his nightgown and paddled in.

'Don't stay in one place too long,' I warned him. 'It sucks you in.'

'Mmm, it *is* a bit soft,' he said, swinging the rake into a thick black mess of leaves and twigs.

'I don't know why I bother really,' I said.

'Ah,' said God, 'leave it this year, you know, it'll be twice as bad next.'

'It's like the gardening,' I said. 'All weeds and backache. Never-ending battle.'

God leaned on his rake, surveying the adjacent wilderness of docks and nettles.

'It's your creation,' I said to him. 'Whyn't you keep it tidy?'

'It's *your* garden,' he said. 'Your world, in fact.'

'Mine?' I said.

'On permanent loan,' he explained.

'Thanks,' I said, as if I really wanted it. I suppose I *do* really. 'But don't you care if we let it go to rack and ruin?' I said.

He glided down gently into a stooping position as the rake sank beneath him. 'Isn't this fun?' he said.

'You be serious,' I said. 'This discussion has implications.'

'Is that catching?' said God. 'I do hope not.'

He was still sinking with the rake, bent double, hair and beard both hanging in the water.

'There are days,' I observed, 'when you are frustratingly inscrutable.'

'In what?' he said, head upside-down.

'Inscrutable.'

'Ah!' he said. 'My view of the world is from quite a different angle to yours.'

'I'm not surprised in that position,' I said. 'The way things are, though, there'll soon be nothing left to view.'

He straighted up. 'You're not planning to blow it up?' he asked.

56

'I'm scared stiff someone else might,' I told him.

'Really?' he said, 'I thought all the arguments were against it?'

I said, 'What?'

'Pressing the nuclear button,' he went on. 'It's no Great Deterrent if no one really means to use it. Why bother?'

'It's employment,' I said.

'Don't be cynical,' said God.

'It's the uncertainty that's worrying,' I said.

'The mistrust, you mean,' God said. 'You know, *you'd* be offended if people said they didn't trust *you*.'

'All right,' I said, 'so none of us can be trusted. If *you're* so reliable, why don't you *do* something?'

'I'm too trusting, I suppose,' said God, 'I was relying on you.'

'Me?'

'Well,' he added, 'You and a few million others.'

'You can see for yourself how pointless that is,' I said. 'Totally ineffectual. The stockpiles of rockets, missiles, bombs – they just go on increasing. Nothing ordinary people can do. Can't you make the world see sense?'

'Oh, it does!' he said emphatically. 'But seeing's not believing, is it?'

I said, 'Isn't it?'

'You see sense,' he said, 'and do different. It'll work out though. People's stupidity catches up with them sooner or later.'

'That's all very well,' I said, 'but the innocent get hurt in the process.'

'It's the only way to make people care,' he said.

'But *you* don't, 'I insisted. 'Or you'd *do* something. The world's just one big mess!'

He seemed distracted. 'I've got a problem here,' he said. His rake had caught in a tangle of old barbed wire and tree branches. He seemed to be losing a fierce tug-of-war with it.

'One good tug should do it,' I said. 'Come on. Pull!'

We heaved together. And together, as the wire sprang suddenly free, spraying water and twanging dangerous loose ends about, we

toppled backwards into the dyke.

'Just look at us,' I said.

'Covered in muck and glory,' said God.

You couldn't help laughing. 'I suppose you'll be telling me next you can't have one without the other.'

'I might,' he answered, 'It's true. The bigger the mess, the greater the glory.'

I said, 'Glory?'

'Sense of achievement,' God said. 'And survival.'

I fingered the black ooze that we sat in. '*This* is survival?'

'I'm right in it with you,' said God. 'How can it be anything else?'

And we laughed some more.

Holy Potato

There's nothing like a good soak and a song from an old movie: 'I'm singing in the baa-th, just singing in the baaaaa-th. . . .'

Or a rousing hymn. With the aid of soap and flannel I was going through my repertoire: 'Holey, holey, ho – oley, all my socks are ho – oley. . . .'

'You're at it again,' said God, arriving without so much as a knock at the door.

'What?' I said.

'Making fun of religion,' he said.

I sang on regardless: 'Holey, holey, holey . . . Do you know, I've got a hole in my shoe as well?' I said. 'Lets the water in.'

'You're not wearing shoes in the bath?'

'Course not,' I said. 'I mean when I'm out in the rain. Just the one shoe. I have to walk with a limp to stop the wet coming in . . . Holey, holey, holey . . .'

'Must be something more holy than socks and shoes,' said God.

'Cullenders,' I said.

'You're very quick tonight,' he said, 'but I'm not spelling *holy* the way you're spelling it.'

'Well, that's *wholly* up to you.' I said.

'Oh, give over,' said God, 'I didn't drop in just to listen to you being witty.'

'What do you want then?' I asked.

'You'll see,' he said. 'Pull the plug out and dry up. I'll go and put the kettle on.'

'You don't mean *dry up*, you mean. . .'

'*I* know what I mean,' said God.

When I was dressed, I found him in the front room with coffee and biscuits on a tray. I settled down opposite him in a comfortable chair.

'This is what's holy,' said God.

'Coffee and biscuits?' I said. 'What are they – chocolate holy-meal?'

'Oh dear me,' said God. 'You get worse.'

He really meant it, so I shut up.

'A simple meal, shared with a friend,' he said. 'Isn't that holy?'

'Well, maybe if we'd said grace over them first,' I said, dimmer than ever.

There was a long silence then, as though a wall had come between us. I wasn't sure who'd built it.

Suddenly it was down again, and God was rushing me out of the door.

'Never mind the biscuits, let's go down the Chip Shop,' he said.

The speed with which he sometimes leaps from one thing to another often leaves me gasping. I followed him down the street, almost running.

'Let's have 'em open,' he said, 'and walk along the sea-front.'

'So it's chips now, is it?' I said, beginning, possibly, to see where our earlier conversation had been leading.

The smell in the Chip Shop was irresistibly appetizing. God ordered two portions, open.

'Salt and vinegar?' he asked.

'Holy delicious,' I said. 'What's next? Holy mackerel?'

'They've only got cod,' said God.

We took our chips, feeling their heat through the wrapping paper, and strolled along the front under the swaying illuminations, enjoying the fresh air and the smell of the sea.

'It's amazing what you can do with a common potato,' I said, holding up a chip and examining it, 'Chipped, mashed, creamed, baked, sauté, stuffed. And crisps too.'

'Not so common, then, is it?' said God.

'Course it is,' I said. 'It's plain and ordinary, basic and plentiful. If that's not common, I don't know what is.'

'All depends how you look at it,' said God. 'I'd call it simple, useful, unassuming and humble. That's not common. That's rare and precious.'

'You wouldn't mean *holy* by any chance?' I ventured to say.

'What's holy?' he asked.

'Well,' I began, 'before you came along, I might have said things like church, prayers and silence, choirs singing, religious ceremony and tradition.'

'Holy?' he said. 'Why?'

'They're special,' I said, 'Set apart for your use.' But I knew he was leading me further. I wasn't sure I could keep up with him.

'And what is this quality you call holiness?' he said.

'Not sure,' I said. 'It's a sort of intrinsic purity and inner cleanliness.'

'Like a dose of liver salts?' he said.

'Don't put me off,' I said. 'I'll get there, eventually. Holiness is . . . reverence and respect, purity, perfection . . . separation from all that's evil and corrupting.'

'Untouched by human hand?' God said.

61

'Well, I don't know, sort of, I suppose.' He'd got me floundering. How can you put the inexpressible into words? 'It's what *you* are,' I suggested finally.

'You think I'm some kind of disinfectant,' God said, 'but you're right about one thing. Holiness is special. What you call common is simply what you take so much for granted you belittle and despise it. True holiness is the value you remember to give those things.'

'Do I really take so much for granted?' I asked him.

'Home, family, health, food, people, talents, work. . . .'

'Don't go on,' I said, 'I get the message. The holiness of ordinary things. I'll try to remember.'

'Good,' said God. 'Have a chip – untouched by human hand.'

'You sure?' I asked.

'No,' said God, 'but *I've* touched it.'

God's Lib

I was ironing some decent creases into a clean pair of trousers when God arrived.

'Quite the little housewife,' he said.

'Well, either *I* press 'em, or I wear 'em crumpled,' I said.

'You mean, *she* won't do 'em?' said God.

'They're *my* trousers,' I answered.

'I see,' said God, 'What you call Women's Lib, is it? If men wear the trousers, they have to press 'em.'

'No,' I said. 'Women's Lib is about men *not* wearing the trousers.'

'Interesting,' said God.

'What I mean is,' I tried to explain, 'it's about fair shares, equal opportunities, equal pay for equal work, neither sex wearing the trousers.'

'More interesting than ever,' said God.

'It's just a figure of speech,' I said, 'though I'll try to avoid it in future. You're becoming indelicate.'

'I should move your iron as well,' he said, 'or you'll have no trousers to wear at all.'

'Oh shut up!' I said.

'You think pressing trousers is women's work,' he went on. 'That's why you're irritable.'

'Make yourself useful, can't you?' I snapped. 'Make some tea or something. I could do with a cup.'

'What?' said God. 'Me? Women's work?'

'God,' I said, 'what are you going on about?'

His reply was instant. His voice was pitched unusually high, and he spat out the words like a catalogue of terrible instruments from a Black Museum: 'Slaving over a hot stove, up to my elbows in suds, hoovering, dusting, running up curtains, changing nappies. . . .'

'Wait a minute!' I said, but he didn't.

'Ironing, sewing, shopping. Oh! That terrible trudge round Tesco's. . . .'

'Stop babbling on,' I said. 'Let me get a word in.'

But he just changed course. 'Coal-mining, bus-driving, sand-blasting, brick-laying, tree-felling. . . .'

'What do *you* know about it?' I shouted.

He stopped. His look said, 'Everything,' but he didn't say it. He looked thoughtful, even mischievous. Then he said, 'I'll show you.' And he did.

She was tall, attractive, dark-haired. She wore God's nightgown, or one extremely like it, but to say the least, she filled it rather differently.

'Where's God gone?' I said.

'Does every mystery have to be explained?' she said, 'Just be grateful.'

'Why?' I said. 'What did you have in mind?'

She smiled. 'I'll make some tea if you like.'

'Good, yes, good idea,' I said. 'I'll just press the pockets, then I've done. Worst bit, the pockets.'

'The thing is,' she said, setting out cups on a tray, 'men and women ought to treat each other as though they were *people*.'

'They *are* people,' I said.

'God knows that,' she said, 'but men and women hang labels round each other's necks – breadwinner, handyman, father: home-maker, sex-object, mother. Nobody's got the imagination to see that the labels are interchangeable.'

'Most of the time they're not,' I said. 'Take you and me. We're different, biologically, emotionally. God discriminated from the beginning. Male and female created he them.'

'So he did,' she answered. 'Different in body, but alike in soul. That's what makes it possible for a man and woman to become one with each other and with him in an act of love and creation.'

'You mean *sex*,' I said.

'I mean sex,' she said, 'and tenderness and respect and com-munion on a level way beyond the mere mechanics of it.'

'You mean, if I should look upon you as a sex object. . . .'

'*Any* kind of object,' she interrupted, 'household or otherwise.'

I wondered how that left me. I didn't want to be an object either. Couldn't *I* be a person, too? I got quite worked up.

'I don't want to be taken for granted, either,' I said. 'My work's got routine and drudgery too, you know!'

'Steady,' she said. 'Did you think you were talking to someone else?'

'No,' I said, 'I wouldn't talk to her like that. Life's got its share of chores for both of us, man and wife.'

65

We drank the tea and sat for a little while longer, just talking.

'It's everybody's lib really,' she said.

'What is?' I asked her.

'Women's Lib,' she said. 'It's men's lib, children's lib. God's lib. It's freedom. It's anyone's.'

'Freedom from what?' I said.

'From tradition, prejudice, narrow-mindedness, selfishness. All sorts!' she said.

She got up, then, and I followed her into the kitchen with the tray. At least, I thought I did.

I found God at the sink, the sleeves of his nightgown rolled up, squirting Sudsy Liquid into the washing-up bowl.

'Where've you been?' I said.

'Having tea with a friend,' he answered.

For a moment I didn't know what to say. 'You mean . . . she. . .?'

'I know,' he said. 'You're wondering what on earth you're going to say next time you're in church and the minister begins "Our *Father*".'

I was staggered by the possibilities: 'Er . . . what shall I say? Mother? Daughter? Sister? Auntie?. . . Girl-friend?'

'Father'll do,' said God. 'Your own needs will make the appropriate translation. Are you drying these pots or not? I'm running out of draining board.'

'Do you know?' I said. 'You sounded just like my wife then.'

God didn't look up from the sink, but I fancy if I could have heard him smiling, the noise would have deafened me.

Chip off the Block

The man in the wood yard looked familiar.

'Got any three-quarter shelving?' I said.

'What you making?' he said. 'Three-quarters of a shelf?'

'You know what I mean,' I said, and gave him a note with the measurements on.

'Shan't be long,' he said, but I stopped him.

'Don't I know you from somewhere?'

'Don't think so,' he said.

'You've shaved your beard off,' I said, 'but I know the face.'

'Dad's got a beard,' he said. 'Perhaps it's him, you know. He's in the office. I'll go and cut your timber.'

When I put my head round the office door I saw how the mix-up had occurred. There was the face I knew. God's face. He was sitting at a desk checking invoices.

'Hello,' he said. 'What can I do for you?'

'I just met your son out there,' I said.

'You mean Jack?' said God.

I said, 'Jack? Don't you mean. . .?'

'No,' said God. 'Not Jesus of Nazareth, Jack, from Biggleswade.'

'He said he was your son,' I insisted.

'Isn't everyone?' said God, 'Our Father, and all that. Or a daughter, of course.'

'Oh, I see,' I said, disappointed. 'I thought for a minute I'd met somebody special.'

'The *real* Jesus?' said God.

I nodded.

'They killed him,' he said.

'I've read the story,' I said, 'in the Bible. Malicious it was; cruel and pointless. Tragic end to a good life.'

I must have said something amiss, I decided. God frowned, and the point of his pencil tore a hole in one of the invoices.

'Well,' I said, trying to make amends but remain honest, 'it's hard to believe in his coming back to life.'

'You don't have to if you don't want to,' said God.

I wasn't shocked. I think I know God well enough now to twig when he's purposely trying to turn my thinking inside out. It's usually for my own good.

Anyway, two can play at that game, I thought. So I said, 'All right then, I won't.' And I left him to his invoices.

Jack had the wood ready. 'That's £4.50 plus VAT,' he said. 'Pay at the office.'

'I've just been in there,' I said. 'Your father's playing up again.'

'Letting you choose what you believe, is he? He's never been any different, you should know that.'

'Doesn't make it easy,' I said.

'I know,' said Jack, 'This Jesus feller – he's all so long ago and far away.'

'He's supposed to be alive *now*,' I said. 'That's the problem.'

'No problem,' answered Jack, 'Mystery, if you like. Life needs mysteries. God wouldn't be God without them.'

'So he *is* dead.'

'Depends . . .' said Jack. 'If you ask me, he was one of those brilliant ideas in God's mind that took shape in a human body. The body died all right, but the idea's far from dead.'

'So it's just a story, then?' I said.

I could almost feel the effort Jack was putting into being patient with me. He changed tack. 'What are you going to make with this wood?' he asked.

'Shelves,' I told him.

'Got a picture of 'em in your mind, have you?'

'Yes,' I said.

'Trust your plans and measurements do you? Nails? Screws? Your own skill?' he went on.

'Look!' I said. 'It's hardly an act of faith, putting up shelves. I'm not moving mountains! Experience, that's all it needs!'

'Right on,' said Jack. 'Imagination and experience puts up shelves.'

'And it makes Jesus real,' said God, overhearing and coming to the door. 'There's not a lot to choose between an event that happens in the mind and one that happens in history. One's as real as the other if it makes a significant difference to the way you live.'

I wondered if that was really so. 'Just suppose,' I said, 'that I settled the bill for this timber *in my mind*. I could walk out of here without paying.'

God said, 'Lies are still lies, and truth is still truth, even if you think it's all in the mind. It still makes a difference to the kind of person you are.'

I wasn't sure if we were still talking about Jesus of Nazareth. It seems we were.

'Someone,' said God, 'had to face the evil represented by so many of the inhabitants of this world.'

'It killed him,' said Jack.

'But we don't *have* to be like it,' I said. 'We don't have to crucify him over and over again. Why don't you *make* us like *him*?'

'I *did*,' said God. 'He could have chosen differently. He had the same freedom that you have.'

'And *I* choose badly. Is that it?'

God looked at Jack. Jack looked at God. Then they both looked at me. I felt guilty.

'But he was your *son. You* lived in *him*,' I cried.

And God said, 'There's as much of me packed into you as it's possible to pack into a human being. You only have to let it *live*.'

That was hard to take. Does anyone know what makes him tick? Who he really is?

I said, 'Who? *Me*?'

And God said, 'You, *my son*.'

Odds on God

There's no sense stepping out into the road just to miss walking under a ladder. It was leaning against a house-front with less than an inch of pavement between the bottom of it and the road. I walked under it.

'You're not superstitious, then?' a voice called down. I recognized it at once.

'God,' I said, 'it's you. I might have known. What are you doing up there?'

'Coming down,' said God. 'It's tea-break.'

Supping tea from the flask he pulled out of an old kit-bag resting by the wall, we sat together on the pavement.

'Nice shade o' brown it is,' God said. 'Would have gone with your eyes.'

I must have looked puzzled.

'The paint,' he said. 'If I'd dropped it on you from up there. That would ha' been a spot o' bad luck.'

'Walking under ladders?' I said. 'If I'd stepped out into the road, I might've got knocked down. What would that have been?'

'A nasty accident,' said God.

'*And* stupid,' I said. 'Anyway, what's bad luck? If it's not an accident, it's your own fault. Under ladders, broken mirrors, spilt salt – superstitious bunkum!'

'I know,' said God.

'Course you do.' I said, 'I don't know why you let me go on so.'

'No?' he said. Then I found out.

'You thinking of giving up religion?' he asked.

'I never said that.'

'As good as,' he insisted. ''S'full o' superstition after all. . . .'

His eyes glistened.

'All those beads and statues and crucifixes. . . .'

'That's not superstition,' I said.

'All that standing up and kneeling down, and bobbing and nodding and wearing of collars back to front. . . .' He muttered away as though he was going on for ever. 'All that performing with bread and wine, candles and water, parading and chanting. . . .'

'Will you let me get a word in edgeways?' I shouted.

But he droned on, the innocence of a devil's advocate shining in his face.

'Close your eyes,' he sang, 'and put your hands together.' He matched his words with the actions. 'And see what the fairies will bring you!'

'You've gone too far this time,' I shouted, frightening a pigeon that had perched on a rung of the ladder. 'Of *all* the people I would expect to have to justify the customs of the church to, you're the *last*. You *know* why we do these things.'

'Oh, *I* know,' said God, with a smile. 'But do *you?*'

'You need symbols,' I said.

'Oh, is there going to be a percussion band?' said God.

'You might have resisted that one,' I told him. 'You know what I mean. Pictures, visual aids, the props and theatre of religion that present the faith in concrete terms.'

He was quiet for a bit then, listening instead of interrupting, so I went on. 'It's not the words, the statues or the traditions we put our faith in, it's *you.*'

'Really?' he said.

'Who else?' I asked.

'What for?' he said.

I asked myself what for. Direction? Security? Meaning? Before I'd arrived at any conclusion he'd spoken again.

'How'd you know about me, anyway?' he said.

'Oh,' I said, 'an assortment of evidence – no, perhaps not evidence – feelings, a response to something outside, or even inside me.'

'The Bible?' God put in.

'Perhaps,' I said. 'There's more to you than you can read in any book.'

'Thanks,' God said. 'What else?'

And while I was thinking, he vanished. Pfft! Gone!. . . . But his voice had not gone. 'What else then?' the voice said, all distant and hollow. 'An apparition? A ghost? A figment? *A nothing*?'

It was unnerving. 'Come back,' I said, '*I'm* nothing without you.'

'Grow up,' said the voice. 'You don't need *me*.'

'Without you,' I said, 'I can't grow at all.'

'You mean you want that white-haired, whiskery cartoon character to come back? To put your *faith* in?'

I had to think about that. That caricature of God *was* a bit like an old plank – familiar, reassuring, supportive – like a floorboard, but no more, really, than a piece of theological wreckage washed up on the beach. Far out, under the waves, there were greater depths to be explored.

'How did I get here?' I gasped suddenly, looking down at the rolled up bottoms of my trousers and feeling the wet sand between my toes. The old man was up to his tricks again. I stared out across the broad expanse of sea and God's voice seemed to roll towards me on the waves.

'Want me to come back?' he said again.

'You're right,' I said. 'You're just a caricature; a picture to hold you in my mind, to make you real and graspable.'

'A symbol?' said the voice.

'More,' I said. 'A stepping stone, a bridge on the way to finding out what you really are.'

'A superstition then,' he said, but I refused to rise to the bait.

'Superstition,' I said, 'I can take it or leave it. But *you're* a mystery. *That's* irresistible.'

Sometimes I think that God lets us do no more than paddle in the shallow, white fringes of his deep, deep waters.